How To Be Blessed By God

Keith A. Butler Sr.

Unless otherwise indicated, all Scripture quotations in this volume are from the *King James Version* of the Bible.

Scripture taken from *The Amplified Bible*, Old Testament copyright © 1965, 1987 by the Zondervan Corporation. The Amplified New Testament copyright © 1958, 1987 by The Lockman Foundation. Used by permission.

First Printing 2001

ISBN 1-893575-10-1

Word of Faith Publishing
20000 W. Nine Mile Road
Southfield, MI 48075-5597

Contents

1. What It Means To Be Blessed 1

2. Cooperate With God
    And Get in the Flow of His Blessings! 5

3. Walking in the Fear
    And the Favor of God 19

4. Your Decisions Will Direct Your Destiny 35

5. Staying in the Flow of God's Blessings 57

6. Be Devoted to God
    And Abound in His Blessings! 79

Chapter 1
What It Means To Be Blessed

The Word of God shows us everything we need to know to be blessed by Him. We don't have to be envious of others who are blessed. We don't have to try to connive and scheme in order to be blessed. No, God's Word provides us with the guidelines we need to be richly blessed by God. If you will act on the truths revealed from the Word within this book, you will not only be blessed, but you will also become a huge blessing in the lives of many!

Let's first find out from the Word of God why we should care about being blessed.

> **PROVERBS 10:22**
> 22 The blessing of the Lord, it maketh rich, and he addeth no sorrow with it.

If you look up the word rich in the Hebrew, you will find that it means *to accumulate*. Or we could say it means *to grow rich* and *to make yourself rich*. So, in other words, the blessing of the Lord causes us to accumulate and it causes us to make ourselves rich. I also want you to notice that the blessing of the Lord never brings sorrow with it.

When God blesses you, it will lift you up. And it won't be a "mixed bag" of lifting you up and then putting you down. You know, God has been accused of all kinds of things, such as putting sickness and disease on people. He has also been accused of doing things to bring people down and then blessing them to lift them up. No! The blessing of the Lord makes rich, and there is no sorrow attached to it!

'Blessing' Defined

Now what does it mean, *"The blessing of the Lord..."* (Prov. 10:22)? What does the word bless or blessing mean? It's a highly overused word that people use all the time but don't really know what it means. It's like the word "grace." That's a religious word that people have a general understanding about, but they don't know specifically what it means. Well, the word bless is the same way.

I'm going to give you several definitions for the word bless because there are several different Hebrew words for "bless" in the Scripture. There are also several different *Greek* words for "bless." We need to know which is which. If we want to be blessed by God, we need to know what it means to be blessed! We also need to know what to do to have God's blessing come about in our lives.

One definition of "bless" in the Hebrew language is *to kneel*. "Bless" also denotes *God blessing man as a benefit*. Another definition is *benediction*. That word benediction means that there is a pronouncement at the end of something. At a ceremony, for example, you would pronounce the benediction at the closing. You're pronouncing, "That's the end." Then you go home. The same is true in a church service. When there is a "benediction," that will be the end of the service.

Well, the word blessing in Proverbs 10:22 refers to God pronouncing a benediction. He is saying, "That's it. This is the end of their poverty and the beginning of their blessing."

The word blessing also means *prosperity*. Another definition of "blessed" is *happy* (or "*how happy*"!). If you're looking for happiness, you will find it in God's blessing.

Other Hebrew meanings for "blessed" are *to be straight*; *to be level*; *to be right*; *to be forward*; *to be honest*.

Some of the Greek definitions for the word bless or blessed are *to speak well of*; *to invoke a benediction upon*; *to prosper*; and *to be fortunate and well off*. In other words, when we're talking about being blessed by God, we're talking about being fortunate. We're talking about being well off. We're talking about being prosperous. We're talking about God having declared a benediction or saying, "This is the end of their having to deal with whatever the enemy is bringing against them. I pronounce blessing upon them."

When you're talking about being blessed, you're talking about God touching every area of your life. You're talking about how happy you are! The world is looking for happiness. They've tried to find it in drink. They've tried to find it in the opposite sex. They've tried to find it in money. They've tried to find it in all kinds of things. But the truth is, none of these things produces blessing. Blessings come from the Lord, and the blessing of the Lord makes us to be rich with no sorrow attached to it.

Chapter 2
Cooperate With God and Get In the Flow of His Blessings!

There are things we can do that will cause prosperity to come to us. There are things we can do to be happy, well off, and well spoken of. As I began to study this subject, I found fifteen different things in the Word of God that cause His blessings to follow us or that produce God's blessings in our life. Let's take a look at them.

Number One:
Learn How To Endure Temptation

When you put yourself in a position to be blessed, you put yourself in position for overflow. You put yourself in position for it to be "your year." The *first* way to set yourself up for God's blessing is *to endure temptation*.

> **JAMES 1:12**
> **12 Blessed is the man that ENDURETH TEMPTA-TION: for when he is tried, he shall receive the crown of life, which the Lord hath promised to them that love him.**

The individual who will not give up and quit, though he is tempted, tested, and tried, is the individual who is putting himself in a position to be blessed. The word "blessed" here in James 1:12 means *to invoke a benediction*; *to speak well of or upon*; and *to prosper*. The individual who endures temptation will be well spoken of by God.

If you will endure temptation, you will prosper. "Temptation" means *temptations, tests, and trials.* Did you know that even though God intends for this to be your year and even though overflow is coming your way, the enemy of your soul will not sit there and just let you walk into it. He's going to attempt to fight you every step of the way. So if you learn how to endure temptation, you will be blessed.

In other words, you're going to have to make up your mind and say, "I'm getting what God has for me and that's all there is to it! And there is nothing that can stop me from getting it!" You have to have that kind of mindset.

Now if you have that mindset and you are willing to endure temptations, tests, and trials, victory is yours regardless of what the enemy brings your way. If you "hang in there" with the Word of God, you will prosper. That's a promise of God we just read in James 1:12. And you can stand boldly and confidently on the promise of God. If it's in the Word, you can stand on it: *"Heaven and earth shall pass away, but God's Word will stand forever"* (Matt. 24:35). Certainly, then, if earth is still here, you know you can count on what you read in God's Word!

When you stand on the Word, you will be blessed. The devil cannot win. Whatever he brings your way will not prosper. Instead, you will be the one that prosperity comes to.

Let's look at the *second* thing in the Word of God that causes us to be blessed.

Number Two:
Begin With the Word of God

The *second* thing we can do to be blessed is *to begin with the Word of God.* Being blessed doesn't start with how you feel about a matter or with what you think about a matter. No, being blessed starts with the Word of God. It starts with, "Let me find out what God says about the matter." Let's read from the Book of James.

JAMES 1:25
25 But whoso looketh into the PERFECT LAW OF LIBERTY, and CONTINUETH therein, he being

**not a forgetful hearer, but a doer of the work,
this man shall be BLESSED in his deed.**

What man (or woman) is it that will be blessed or prosperous in his deed? The man (or woman) who does two things: 1) *looks into the perfect law of liberty*; and 2) *continues therein.*

First, the person who is blessed in his deed looks into the perfect law of liberty. The law of liberty or freedom is the Word of God. Notice it's called the *law* of liberty. It's called a law because it always works.

The definition of a law is that it works. It works all the time. For example, there's the law of gravity. It doesn't matter what you feel about the law of gravity; if you get on top of a building and jump off, you're going to find out about that law! People can tell you that it won't work, but it will work! I guarantee you that if you jump off a building that's tall enough, we will end up scraping you off the ground! That's because of the law of gravity — the law of gravity works!

Well, there is another law — the law of liberty, the law of freedom — the Word of God. The Word of God always works. It always works under the conditions of someone looking into it and then continuing in it.

James 1:25 says, ". . . *whoso LOOKETH into the perfect law of liberty, and CONTINUETH therein. . . .* " The word "continueth" means that this is something you do every day. This is something you don't stop doing. You're in the Word of God all the time. You're in it on Sunday, Monday, Tuesday, Wednesday, Thursday, Friday, and Saturday. You continue in the Word because you want to see what God has to say about your situation, and you want to continue in that.

Being blessed by God comes not by just *looking* into the Word — into the perfect law of liberty — but by *continuing* in the Word.

It doesn't matter whether you're an accountant, an engineer, a housewife, or a househusband — if you start out with the Word of God every day, you put yourself in position to have the prophetic Word work in your life and make you prosperous.

Let's find out what else you can do to put yourself in position to be blessed.

Number Three:
Act on the Word of God

Remember that James 1:25 talks about being a "doer of the work."

JAMES 1:25
**25 But whoso looketh into the perfect law of liberty,
and continueth therein, he being not a forgetful
hearer, but a DOER OF THE WORK, this man shall
be blessed in his deed.**

The *third* thing you need to do to be blessed is *to
act on the Word of God*. Whatever you find in the
Word of God, you need to act on it. You have to
decide that you're going to do it. Again, it has nothing to do with how you feel or what you think. For
example, if God's Word says to love those who use
you despitefully (and it does say that), then you're
going to have to do it.

Matthew 6:44 says, *". . . pray for them which
despitefully use you, and persecute you."* That means
that, to act upon that, you're going to have to spend
time praying for that person who hurt you. You're
going to have to pray for that individual who caused
other thoughts besides love thoughts to come to your
mind! But God said that if you do it, you will be
blessed!

Now the blessings of the Lord cause an individual
to prosper. They make rich, and there won't be any
sorrow with them. You'll find that when you do
something God's way, it will produce something good
in your life. And it will produce quickly! It will pro-

duce an abundant overflow, and you won't have to wait years for it to happen. When you're positioning yourself to be blessed by God, you can say, "This is my year!"

We understand that, although God wants to bless you, He can only go as far with you as you let Him. In other words, you have to *cooperate* with God for Him to be able to do the full extent of what He desires to do for you. Now the Father will go as far as He can with you, but whether you receive one hundred percent of all the blessings in His Word is up to you. If you're going to act on twenty-five percent of the Word, then you're going to get a twenty-five-percent blessing. If you're going to do fifty percent, then you're going to get a fifty-percent blessing.

But if you will act on the Word all the way, you will get a one hundred-percent blessing. And one hundred percent is what's available to you!

Number Four: Listen to God

Well, what's the *fourth* thing that causes God to be able to bless you? *Listening to Him.* Notice what God said in the Book of Proverbs.

> **PROVERBS 8:32-34**
> **32 Now therefore hearken unto me, O ye children: for blessed are they that keep my ways.**
> **33 Hear instruction, and be wise, and refuse it not.**

**34 Blessed is the man that heareth me, watching
daily at my gates, waiting at the posts of my door.**

We are told in this passage that an individual is
blessed who listens to God: *"Now therefore HEAR-
KEN unto me. . . "* (v. 32). "Hearken" means *to listen unto.* God said, "Listen to what I'm telling you."
It's one thing to hear God; it's another thing to
hearken unto or listen to Him. (You can hear God
and refuse to listen. I'm going to talk more about
that in this book.)

Now you have to take time to listen. You have
to decide, "I'm not going to just run off and do what
I think should happen. I'm going to do what the
Word of God tells me to do. I'm going to listen to
God. I'm going to acknowledge Him in all my ways
and allow Him to direct my path [Prov. 3:6].

"That means I'm not going to just charge out
and buy the first car I find. I'm not going to jump
at the first house I like. I'm not going to grab the
first boyfriend (or girlfriend) I think is good. I'm
not going to take that promotion and leave town
right away without waiting on the Lord and getting some instruction from Him.

"Before I do anything else, I'm going to 'hearken.' I'm going to take the time to get before God
and listen to the Holy Ghost speak to my spirit. I'm

going to spend time meditating in the Word of God and getting quiet before the Lord so that I can hear Him. If I have to, I'm going to push the plate back and spend some time in fasting and prayer. I'm going to let my mind and my body become quiet. I'm going to listen to God."

Don't Refuse the Instruction God Gives

Notice what else God said. Proverbs 8:33 says, *"Hear instruction, and be wise, and refuse it not."* Why did God say this? Because sometimes what the Lord will say to you will not be what you want to hear. For example, when you get before God at times and start talking to Him about someone who's giving you trouble, the Lord will turn the spotlight and start talking to you about *you.* You might be saying, "Lord, You need to get my husband straightened out." But the Lord says to you, "I will after I get you straightened out."

I've noticed that many times people will ask me, "What does God's Word say about such-and-such a matter?" I will get out the Bible and read God's Word to them. But what I've found is that what they were looking for was for the Bible to agree with them. When they found that it didn't, they said, "Forget the Bible. I'm doing what I want to do anyway."

What were these people doing? They were refusing instruction. And by refusing instruction, they were putting themselves in position to miss the blessing of God. To receive the blessing of God, you must accept all the instructions God gives you — whether you like them or not, whether you understand them or not, or whether you agree with them or not. If you find something in the Word of God, you must make a decision to obey it — to humble yourself under the mighty hand of God enough to trust Him so He can exalt you in due time (1 Peter 5:5,6). You have to hear and listen.

Proverbs 8:34 says, *"Blessed is the man that heareth me. . . ."* We must develop a sense of being able to hear God. That takes time. I remember when I first got saved, I used to hear people say, "Well, the Lord told me this" and "The Lord told me that." I thought, *How come God never speaks to me?* I didn't hear anything from God.

I hadn't had any teaching in this area, so I thought, *I'm going to pray, and then I'm going to stop and listen to see what God says.* I was trying to hear God with my physical ears! But you don't hear God with your physical ears — you hear God in your spirit. And He will speak to you and give you instructions. He will lead you by His Word, His peace, or by the voice of the Holy Ghost speaking to you on the inside, in your spirit.

The Spirit of the Lord will tell you what to do and when to do it. If you're going to operate in the abundant overflow — if this is going to be your year — you're going to have to first slow down and find out what your instructions are. Be excited about spending time with God to find out what you're supposed to do! Have a sense of joyful anticipation. Then hear and listen.

You Can Have a Right Heart And Wrong Instruction

I tell you, more people mess up their blessing, although they have a right heart, because they don't have the right instruction. They run off, so to speak, and do certain things, saying, "Lord, I'm doing this — now bless it!"

But God says, "I'm not blessing what *you're* doing. I'm blessing what *I* am doing." God is only blessing what He's doing. And He wants you to get in position and get in His flow, because when you're doing what it is *He* wants, He will bless that. He will cause you to prosper. And when God blesses you — when the One who has all power in His hand causes you to prosper — He will make an end of that which has tried to come against you.

When God is on your side, there is nothing anyone can do about His blessing you!

Let's see what God told the children of Israel concerning His blessing.

DEUTERONOMY 28:1-8
1 And it shall come to pass, if thou shalt HEAR-
KEN DILIGENTLY unto the voice of the Lord thy
God, to observe and to do all his commandments
which I command thee this day, that the Lord thy
God will set thee on high above all nations of the
earth:
2 And ALL THESE BLESSINGS SHALL COME ON
THEE, and OVERTAKE THEE, if thou shalt hear-
ken unto the voice of the Lord thy God.
3 BLESSED shalt thou be in the city, and
BLESSED shalt thou be in the field.
4 BLESSED shall be the fruit of thy body, and the
fruit of thy ground, and the fruit of thy cattle, the
increase of thy kine, and the flocks of thy sheep.
5 BLESSED shall be thy basket and thy store [in
our day, that would be your bank account].
6 BLESSED shalt thou be when thou comest in,
and BLESSED shalt thou be when thou goest out.
7 The Lord shall cause thine enemies that rise up
against thee to be smitten before thy face: they
shall come out against thee one way, and flee
before thee seven ways.
8 THE LORD SHALL COMMAND THE BLESSING
upon thee in thy storehouses [God is the One who
commands the blessings upon you in your storehouses,
plural!]**, and in all that thou settest thine hand**

**unto; AND HE SHALL BLESS THEE in the land
which the Lord thy God giveth thee.**

Where God sends you and in whatever situation
He puts you, He will bless you. It's not just the
preachers that are supposed to be blessed. It's the
housewives, the children, the secretaries, the
accountants, the teachers, and so forth, that are
supposed to be blessed as well! Whatever you do
will be blessed if you hearken unto the voice of the
Lord your God and observe to do what He said!

God said in Deuteronomy 28:2 that all these
blessings shall overtake you. Now when you talk
about being overtaken, you're talking about something catching you and running you over. God's
blessings — His prosperity, His peace, and His joy —
are running you over! The blessings of the Lord
make rich, and there isn't any sorrow with them
(Prov. 10:22). Did you read about any sorrow in the
passage we just read in Deuteronomy chapter 28?
No, there isn't any!

Let's read on in Deuteronomy.

DEUTERONOMY 28:11,12
**11 And the Lord shall make thee plenteous in
goods . . .**
**12 The Lord shall open unto thee his good trea-
sure, the heaven to give the rain unto thy land in
his season, and to bless all the work of thine hand:**

**and thou shalt lend unto many nations, and thou
shalt not borrow.**

God said He would bless you so that you
wouldn't even have to borrow! Now that was for
the children of God *then*, but it's also for the children of God *now*. When God blesses you, you won't
need help. You'll be the one doing the helping. But
I want to remind you that there's an "if" clause in
verse 1: *"And it shall come to pass, IF thou shalt
hearken diligently unto the voice of the Lord thy
God. . . . "* Your blessing depends on whether or not
you cooperate with God.

Chapter 3

Walking in the Fear
And the Favor of God

As I said previously, the blessing of God, the prosperity of God, does not just cover the realm of finances, health, or even spiritual things. The blessing of the Lord covers every area of your existence. And, remember, the blessing of the Lord makes rich without sorrow.

The Blessing of the Lord
Includes His Favor

Let's look in the Fifth Psalm at what else God says about His blessing.

> **PSALM 5:12**
> 12 For thou, Lord, wilt bless THE RIGHTEOUS; with FAVOUR wilt thou COMPASS him as with a shield.

The word "compass" means *to crown*. The Lord crowns the righteous with favor. Well, who are the righteous? The righteous are those who have made a decision to receive Jesus Christ as their Lord and

Savior. Second Corinthians 5:21 says about Jesus, "He who knew no sin was made to be sin for us, that we might be made the righteousness of God in Him." The righteous are those who act like the righteous in that they govern their lives by the Word of God.

What does it mean to find the favor of God? When you have God's favor, you can walk in places that other people cannot. Favor is required where there are limits, doors, locks, and so forth. But you can be favored with the key! You can be given the pass! You can have the clearance to go in and receive what's available in those places God allows you to go.

God crowns the righteous with favor. Because of God's favor, people will help you. Because of God's favor, you'll be able to get things you couldn't get otherwise. Because of the favor of God, people will shake your hand and commend you, saying, "How in the world were you able to accomplish this?"

God will even talk to the sinner and cause the sinner to help you. Why? Because you are the righteous. So you need to be saying what God says about you. You need to be acting like what God said in His Word is true. You are the righteousness of God because of what Jesus did for you (2 Cor. 5:21). And as long as you act like the righteous, you get to walk in favor.

God's favor will cause abundant provision to overtake you. Remember we're talking about what we can do to be blessed by God. We already looked at the following: 1) *Learn how to endure temptation*; 2) *begin with the Word of God*; 3) *act on the Word of God*; and 4) *listen to God and keep His ways.*

Let's continue looking at what we can do to be blessed by God.

Number Five: Walk in the Fear of God

The *fifth* requirement for walking in the fullness of God's blessings is *to walk the fear of God.*

> **PSALM 115:12-14**
> **12 The Lord hath been mindful of us: he will bless us; he will bless the house of Israel; he will bless the house of Aaron.**
> **13 HE WILL BLESS THEM THAT FEAR THE LORD, both small and great.**
> **14 The Lord shall increase you more and more, you and your children.**

Proverbs 8:13 says, *"The fear of the Lord is to hate evil: pride, and arrogancy, and the evil way, and the froward mouth, do I hate."* Someone who walks in the fear of God will hate evil, will not walk in pride, will disdain the evil way, and will not speak anything other than what God says. There are many things in my life that I've never done because I feared God.

Another definition for the fear of God is reverential respect. There ought to be things that should never come out of your mouth and that you'd never do simply because you respect God. There ought to be some things that will never happen with you because you respect God too much! You don't want to disappoint your Heavenly Father; therefore, there are certain things you will not do.

Notice that God will bless both small and great that fear Him (Ps. 115:13). You don't have to be someone special — your name doesn't have to be well known — for God's blessing to come upon you or overtake you. The Lord Himself will increase you more and more! He will increase you more and more! "More and more" is talking about the overflow of God's blessings. Overflow is more than just the flow — it's the overflow!

You see, God will increase you more and more until you come to the place where you've increased so much that you have more than you can use. That's called overflow, and it doesn't stop with you. The Bible says, "You and your children" (Ps. 115:14). If you have minor children, your children's fortunes are connected to your walking in the fear of God.

PSALM 115:15,16
15 Ye are blessed of the Lord which made heaven and earth.
16 The heaven, even the heavens, are the Lord's: but the earth hath he given to the children of men.

God gives the earth and everything in it to His children. He will give you fame. He'll give you joy. He'll give you whatever it is you need in this life.

Let's read a few more scriptures on the fear of God.

PSALM 128:1-6
1 Blessed is every one [That means you!] **that feareth the Lord; that walketh in his ways.**
2 For thou shalt eat the labour of thine hands: happy shalt thou be, and it shall be well with thee.
3 Thy wife shall be as a fruitful vine by the sides of thine house: thy children like olive plants round about thy table.
4 Behold, that thus shall the man be blessed that feareth the Lord.
5 The Lord shall bless thee out of Zion: and thou shalt see the good of Jerusalem all the days of thy life.
6 Yea, thou shalt see thy children's children [God promises you long life]**, and peace upon Israel.**

Now all of these blessings are a result of walking in the fear of God. Proverbs 8:13 says that the fear of the Lord is to hate evil, pride, and the froward mouth. Hate those things and walk in God's way. Love what He loves, and hate what He hates. Do what He said to do.

Let the Word be your constant standard. Don't look at others when you should be looking at God and His Word. Don't look at someone else and decide, "Well, it doesn't appear to be working for him for some reason, so maybe it won't work for me." I don't read anywhere in the Scripture where it says you're to look at someone else to decide whether or not God's Word will work for you. Other people aren't your example; Jesus is your example.

There are people who have used the excuse, "I don't know about all this fearing the Lord business. I know So-and-so, and they're righteous. They're living for God, yet look at the bad things that have happened to them."

But you don't know anything about those people. You don't know if they've been obedient to God or not. You might know that they haven't committed murder, theft, or fornication. But you don't know whether or not they've been obedient to the Holy Ghost. All you see is the outside — what you've observed outwardly — but sometimes the most hard-headed people are the ones sitting in the pew with a Bible in their lap. (You can be lifted up in pride and have a Bible and a notebook in your lap, going through all the right motions that you're supposed to go through in church.)

Don't judge whether or not you ought to obey God by what someone else has or has not done. The Word of God says, in effect, "Everyone who does what God says to do will be blessed" (Ps. 128:1). And they'll see their children's children. I tell you, I'm going to see my grandchildren. And they're going to be like my children — saved, sanctified, filled with the Holy Ghost, blessed, happy, prosperous, and envied by other people! The anointing of God will be on them, and I will get to see what good things God will do with them.

Remember that to fear God is to have tremendous reverential respect for Him.

> **PSALM 112:1**
> **1 Praise ye the Lord. Blessed** [or empowered to prosper] **is the man that feareth the Lord, that delighteth greatly in his commandments.**

Do you want to have the full measure of the Word of God in your life? Then delight greatly in the Word. When you delight greatly in His Word, no one has to force you to read it or meditate on it. Let me give you an example.

I delight greatly in fried chicken. I could eat it every day. I'm talking about my wife's fried chicken, my mama's fried chicken, and my grand-mama's fried chicken! (I may not like your fried chicken.) I could eat fried chicken every day because I delight greatly in it. I don't know why that bird tastes so good to me!

Now I like fried chicken so much, I have to make sure that I don't become a glutton over it. I have to make sure I don't take another piece while everyone else has had only piece, and I've had six! I have to tell my hands, "Stay down. Be civilized. Act like you have manners." And my body usually says, "You delight greatly in that chicken. Get that other piece." Well, similarly, if you delight greatly in the Word of God, someone doesn't have to force you to go to it.

I can tell you one way you know whether or not you like being in the Word of God, and that's by how many times you go to church during the week. If you go to church sometime other than Sunday, you are probably delighting in God's Word. You don't delight greatly in the Word of God if you only get fed once a week. I have to have fried chicken more than once a week! My wife may not cook it more than once a week, but that doesn't mean I eat it only once a week!

Someone who is delighting in the Word is going to get to where the Word is, because they love the

Word so much! They understand that the Word is "sweeter than the honeycomb" (Ps. 19:10). The Word is greater tasting than fried chicken or whatever food it is they like to eat! The Word of God is their daily delight, and it's the instrument that causes them to walk in the fullness of the blessing God has pronounced.

Your Children Shall Be Mighty!

We read Psalm 112:1, which says, "Blessed is the man that feareth the Lord, that delighteth greatly in his commandments." Verse 2 says something else about your blessing affecting your heritage: *"HIS SEED SHALL BE MIGHTY upon earth: the generation of the upright shall be blessed."*

Now I don't know about you, but I couldn't be blessed if my children were all messed up. One of the things that causes me to be a blessed man is that my children are blessed. Making sure that my children are blessed is very important to me! I want all three of them to do exceedingly well. I want them to do better than their father. Why? Because I love them! They came from me.

Now there are some things I can do in the natural, in addition to the spiritual, to ensure that my seed — my children — will be blessed. For example, I never speak badly about their mother. I love and respect my wife, and they respect her, too, in part, because I set the right example.

Even if you're divorced, you need to watch what you say in front of your children about their other parent. Don't ever say anything negative to your children about their mother or father. When you talk badly about a parent to your child, you are saying to them, "You are no good." Why? Your children are half you and half the other parent.

Let's continue reading in Psalm 112.

>   **PSALM 112:3**
>   3 Wealth and riches shall be in his house: and his righteousness endureth for ever.

I like those words "shall be." You can count on "shall be." Well, when you walk in the fear of God, blessings are coming. If they aren't there yet, they're on the way! And when they catch you, they're going to overflow upon you!

>   **PSALM 112:4**
>   4 Unto the upright there ariseth light in the darkness. . . .

What is that talking about — "there ariseth light in the darkness"? It's talking about revelation — revelation from God. Revelation from God is a blessing because it's the truth. Revelation will show up in the darkest hour. When other people don't know what to do, your head doesn't know what to do, and your body doesn't know what to do, God will give you revelation.

Get hold of that! Everyone runs into some darkness at some time or another. When you do, you need revelation to help you see the light and walk in it.

If you're in a dark room where the doors have been shut and the windows drawn, and it's so dark, you can't see your hand in front of your face, you can't see where you're going. You could bump into all kinds of things. But when you have light, you can see where the obstacles are, step around them, and walk out the door into the sunlight.

Notice something else in this verse about the person who fears the Lord.

PSALM 112:4
4 . . . he is gracious, and full of compassion, and righteous.

The man or woman who fears the Lord is gracious and full of compassion. Let's continue to read

about the blessing of the righteous person who
fears God.

> **PSALM 112:5-9**
> **5 A good man sheweth favour, and lendeth: he will
> guide his affairs with discretion.**
> **6 Surely he shall not be moved for ever: the righ-
> teous shall be in everlasting remembrance.**
> **7 He shall not be afraid of evil tidings** [He has no
> fear!]**: his heart is fixed, trusting in the Lord.**
> **8 His heart is established, he shall not be afraid,
> until he see his desire upon his enemies.**
> **9 He hath dispersed** [He's a giver]**, he hath given to
> the poor; his righteousness endureth for ever; his
> horn shall be EXALTED WITH HONOUR.**

Honor is when someone other than yourself has
a high opinion of you. You won't have to have some
great opinion about yourself when God exalts you
with honor. Everyone else will be talking about the
fact that you are a man or a woman of God.

> **PSALM 112:10**
> **10 The wicked shall see it, and be grieved; he shall
> gnash with his teeth, and melt away: the desire of
> the wicked shall perish.**

Wicked people are going to be upset when the
righteous are blessed. They're going to be envious.
They will say, "They are the luckiest people I've
ever seen." But luck doesn't have anything to do

with it! Everything in the earth happens because someone has been operating the law of God or the law of the devil. Someone has been operating by the law of blessing or the law of cursing. In other words, he's been following the light of the Word or going against the Word.

Whether they know it or not, sinners can follow the light of the Word. That's why you sometimes find individuals who are not born again, yet they are blessed. They do things that are in line with the Word of God, and blessings follow. They don't even understand why they are doing what they're doing. For example, many rich people give to the poor, and more money comes to them. They don't know they're acting on the Word. They just call themselves philanthropists. But God says, "You're doing things My way, so I'm going to bless you, even if you're not one of Mine."

That's the way it works in the earth. Luck has nothing to do with the blessings of God. So there's no sense going to the casinos, hoping God will bless you. What does the Bible say about ill-gotten gain? It says you might get it, but you'll probably lose most of it, or it could cost you down the road in some other way (Prov. 1:19; 15:27; 28:8).

Don't you know that if the devil thinks he can hook you, he will actually help you? He'll help you win a lottery, a bet, and so forth. But his goal is not really to help you. People call it good luck when someone wins the lottery, but the man who fears God doesn't have to hope that "chance" will help him. The Word of God says he shall be blessed!

The Blessings of God Are on the Way!

Notice that this man in Psalm 112 is blessed because he delights in the law of God, he fears God, he hates evil, he hates pride, he hates a froward mouth, and he has complete reverential respect for God. That man's seed is blessed. Wealth and riches are in his house. His right-standing endures forever. He is blessed! Any individual who bases his life on the things we've discussed so far is positioning himself to have the Word of God manifested fully in his life.

In Mark 4:8 and 20, we see that some seed produces thirtyfold, other seed produces sixtyfold, and, finally, other seed produces a hundredfold. Why the variance? The degree to which the seed produces depends on the individual sowing the seed. Did the individual put himself in position for the blessing to work in his life? God can only go as far with you as you will allow Him to go.

You can be a Psalm 112 person! I always say to myself, "I'm a Psalm 112 man. I fear the Lord. I love His Word. And everything I see in Psalm 112 belongs to me!"

Whatever your station in life, when God lifts you up, no man can take you down. Whether you're single or married, rich or poor, fat or skinny, black or white or red or yellow — the blessings of God are available to you! If you'll receive His Word and act on it, walking in the fear of the Lord, you will experience His blessings.

The enemy may come against you, but he has to flee (James 4:7). He may come against you one way, but he will flee seven different ways (Deut. 28:7). Why? Because the Lord is on your side, and there's nothing the devil can do to you to harm you (Luke 10:19; 1 Peter 3:13). Romans chapter 8 says, "What shall separate me from the love of God? Shall tribulation? Distress? Famine? Danger? No! In all these things, we are more than conquerors through Him that loved us" (vv. 35-37).

Just shake your head at the devil and say, "There ain't no way! You won't be able to stop this today! God will bless me coming in! He'll bless me going out! He'll bless me in the city!

He'll bless me in the field! He'll bless me in the basket! He'll bless me in my storehouses! And He'll bless me in all that I set my hand unto!" (*See* Deuteronomy 28:1-14.)

That means that when you go to work, you'll be blessed. When you go to pray, you'll be blessed. When you go on vacation, you'll be blessed. When you get home, you'll be blessed. When you take a shower, you'll be blessed. When you eat a meal, you'll be blessed. When you drive your car, you'll be blessed. Whatever you do, you'll be blessed, because the blessings of the Lord are on their way to you!

Chapter 4

Your Decisions Will Direct Your Destiny

I want to emphasize that your being blessed by God doesn't just depend on God; it depends on you and the decisions that you make. For example, what will you do with the truth? Will you act on it or ignore it?

I mentioned in a previous chapter that I have identified fifteen truths in the Word of God which will instruct you on how to be blessed by God. I talked about five ways to be blessed by God: 1) *Learn how to endure temptation*; 2) *begin with the Word of God*; 3) *act on the Word of God and keep acting on it*; 4) *listen to God*; and 5) *walk in the fear of the Lord*.

Let's continue looking at how to be blessed by God.

Number Six: Don't Walk In the Counsel of the Ungodly

Let's read from the Book of Psalms.

PSALM 1:1-6
1 Blessed is the man that walketh not in the counsel of the ungodly, nor standeth in the way of sinners, nor sitteth in the seat of the scornful.

2 But his delight is in the law of the Lord; and in his law doth he meditate day and night.

3 And he shall be like a tree planted by the rivers of water, that bringeth forth his fruit in his season; his leaf also shall not wither; and whatsoever he doeth shall prosper.

4 The ungodly are not so: but are like the chaff which the wind driveth away.

5 Therefore the ungodly shall not stand in the judgment, nor sinners in the congregation of the righteous.

6 For the Lord knoweth the way of the righteous: but the way of the ungodly shall perish.

Let's read verse 1 from *The Amplified Bible.*

PSALM 1:1 (*Amplified*)

1 Blessed (Happy, fortunate, prosperous, and enviable) is the man who walks and lives not in the counsel of the ungodly (following their advice, their plans and purposes), nor stands (submissive and inactive) in the path where sinners walk, nor sits down (to relax and rest) where the scornful (and the mockers) gather.

This verse of Scripture in Psalm 1 starts out with the phrase, "Blessed is the man." So if we look at what comes after that phrase, we will find out the things that cause a person to be blessed.

The word "blessed" in this scripture means *happy; to be envied.* Then it mentions the first thing about a blessed person: He doesn't walk in the counsel of the ungodly. He doesn't follow their advice. The *sixth* thing you can do to be blessed is *to "walk not" in the counsel of the ungodly.*

You shouldn't be getting your advice from a "1-900" number or some psychic hot line. You shouldn't be getting your advice from cards, the horoscope, or a book about the meaning of dreams.

You're not supposed to get your advice from external sources, and you're certainly not supposed to get it from those who don't know God — His way and methods. The way to be blessed is to follow God's ways, God's words, and God's advice. Psalm 1:1 says, "Happy is the man who walks not in the counsel of the ungodly." A person who has the right advice is happy. He's not sad, because he knows he has the right advice. Paraphrased, *The Amplified Bible* says, "Happy, fortunate, prosperous, and enviable is the man who doesn't follow the ungodly's advice, plans, and purposes."

For me, when it comes to a doctor operating on me, I want one who knows the Lord. I don't want a doctor cutting on me who doesn't even believe in God. The same is true for legal advice. I'm not going to take legal advice from an attorney who doesn't believe in God. Anyone who thinks he knows more than everyone else does and that there's no higher power than himself is ignorant. Why would you want to you take advice from a person like that?

Psalm 1:1 says, *"Blessed is the man that walketh not in the counsel of the ungodly, nor standeth in the way of sinners, nor sitteth in the seat of the scornful."* Who are the scornful? They are those who say, "Ah, that Bible stuff doesn't really mean anything. It's all fairy tales and 'hocus-pocus.' Some man wrote the Bible, not God." The scornful will have any number of excuses for why they don't walk in the sound counsel of God. But the person who chooses not to follow the scornful will be blessed and prosperous.

Let's look again at Psalm 1:2: *"But his delight is in the law of the Lord; and in his law* [in God's Word] *doth he meditate day and night."* A person who delights in God's Word and meditates on it shall be like a tree planted by rivers of water (Ps. 1:3). He or she shall be like a tree that's always fresh and has plenty to receive from — foliage to shelter and fruit to nourish and enrich!

God Has a Season for You

Then notice another phrase in Psalm 1:3: "He shall bring forth his fruit in his season." You see, there is a season for you. And God has fruit that's just for you. God has blessings for you, and you will receive them when you meditate on His Word and take His advice instead of the world's.

Let's continue reading in Psalm 1:3: ". . . *his leaf also shall not wither; and whatsoever he doeth shall prosper.*" The man or woman who delights in God's Word is a blessed person whose leaf does not wither. In other words, a blessed person doesn't dry up and blow away! He is not blown away by life. And whatsoever he does shall prosper.

That is God's will for you. But, first, you must decide that God's Word is true and that you don't want to hear or take counsel from anything other than the Word of God. When you walk not in the counsel of the ungodly, it puts you in a position for God to be able to bless and prosper you in whatsoever you do. In other words, when you go to work, you'll prosper. If you go to school, you'll prosper. When you're at home, you'll prosper. When you go to the bank, you'll prosper. When you sing, you'll prosper. When you pray, you'll prosper. Whatever you do will prosper!

Now let's look at the *seventh* thing that causes you to be blessed by God.

Number Seven:
Put Your Complete Confidence in God

Those who are blessed and prosper put their complete trust in the Lord. Let's read Psalm 2:12.

> **PSALM 2:12**
> 12 Kiss the Son, lest he be angry, and ye perish from the way, when his wrath is kindled but a little. BLESSED are all they that PUT THEIR TRUST IN HIM.

The *seventh* thing you can do to be blessed is *to put your complete confidence in God*. You are blessed when you put your trust in Him. You are blessed, and doors will open for you, when you have complete confidence in the hand of the Lord. That means putting your marriage in God's hands. Or if you are single, you must put your single life in God's hands. I tell singles that if they will do that, they'll stop worrying about whether someone is going to marry them or not!

As a single, you have to be happy with yourself first before you can make someone else happy. You can't expect someone to come along and make you happy. You have to be happy before you meet him or her. And if your trust is in the Lord, you won't be in a hurry to get someone now! If you get in a hurry, you could marry the wrong person. And that could be hell on earth!

When you put your trust in God, you also put your finances in His hands. You put your children in His hands. You put everything you have in His hands. You have total confidence and trust in His ability. You know He won't let you down!

Let me tell you something about God. He will never let you down when you put your total trust in Him. Now you may let yourself down, but if you'll get in the Word and stand on it, you can count on God to do what He said He would do! He can be trusted. You may not be able to trust other people, but I know you can trust the Lord!

PSALM 34:8
8 O taste and see that the Lord is good: BLESSED is the man that TRUSTETH IN HIM.

Some people say, "I can't trust something I don't see. I can't see God, so how can I trust Him?" But let me tell you something. You trust a whole lot of things you can't see. In fact, some of the things you can see aren't worth being trusted. For example, you have confidence in man's ability to make things. You sit down in a chair without even considering whether that chair is going to hold you up. You don't have any real evidence that it will. You aren't one-hundred percent positive that it will hold you up. Yet you just "plop" down on that chair, and you don't worry about falling. You don't even think about it. But don't you know that chairs can break? Man makes chairs, and man is fallible. But God is infallible — He never fails.

> **PSALM 40:4**
> 4 Blessed is that man that maketh the Lord his trust, and respecteth not the proud, nor such as turn aside to lies.

The person who makes a decision to trust God rather than man's devices is blessed. Now some men can help you. I mean, they can help you scheme and connive. But the Bible says that as a man sows that shall he also reap (Gal. 6:7). If you connive to get something, you'd better know that your time is coming. You're on the way down. But if God promotes you — if He lifts you up — no one can take you down. And that comes from trusting God.

My Own Step of Faith

I have placed my life in God's hands. When I was working at a secular job and the Spirit of God called me to go into the ministry full-time, I had to put my life in His hands. I had to leave my great job and go to Bible school. Just about the time I was going to be very blessed at my job, God came along and said, "Now I want you to do this. And I want you to quit that job. I want you to go to a place you've never seen before."

God wanted me to go to RHEMA Bible Training Center in Broken Arrow, Oklahoma. I didn't even know where Oklahoma was! I thought, *Oklahoma? Who goes out there?* So I had to make a decision to trust God, because I knew without a doubt that it was the voice of the Lord speaking to me. I guarantee you, it wasn't my idea to quit my job and go to Oklahoma! That was the furthest thought from my mind.

There will come times in life when you will have to "put up or shut up." I mean, you will have to either believe God and put your trust in Him or not believe Him. You have to make up your mind which way it's going to be. If you're going to believe this thing, you'll have to get all the way in!

We were "head over hills" in debt at the time the Lord spoke to me. We knew that if we stayed where we were, we would get out of debt. I was about to come into a promotion and make some real money on that job. We were steeped — up to the gills — in debt! But we knew that in time everything would be all right if I just kept working at my job. But I left it behind to move to Oklahoma with my wife and son and only $264 to my name.

In Oklahoma, we were sitting in Kenneth Hagin Ministries' Campmeeting, and they have one day that's called "RHEMA Day." Brother Kenneth E. Hagin said, "On RHEMA Day, bring a special offering. If you were going to bring one dollar, bring two dollars. Just double-up your offering."

Well, I didn't have much of an offering to give. I didn't even have a job at that point. I'd brought my wife and twelve-month-old son to Oklahoma, leaving family, friends, my job, and everything we had behind. Everyone I knew in Detroit thought I had lost my mind. When I first told certain people about our plans, they laughed in my face. They said, "You're going to follow God and do what? You'll be back before January if you don't starve first, boy."

So I had decided not to give in that special RHEMA offering. But my wife turned to me in the service and said, "I believe the Lord is saying we're to give a hundred dollars."

I looked at her and said, "A hundred dollars! Are you sure?" You have to understand that this was 1977, and $100 was worth more than it is now.

She said, "Yes, the Lord is speaking to us to do that." I checked my spirit to see if I had peace about that. I did, so I ran up to the altar with everyone else and threw the money down. When I got back to my seat, I thought, *Man, this had better work. We need a harvest fast!* Then my wife turned to me and said, "I believe the Lord is saying you're supposed to give another hundred dollars."

I said, "What! Are you sure?"

She said, "Yes." Now all kinds of thoughts were coming to my head: *This woman is crazy. She's lost her mind. Who is this woman You sent me, God? That only leaves us with sixty-four dollars. And I don't have a job! You've got to be kidding.*

Finally, I checked my spirit, and she was right. I looked at her, and she was looking at me as if to say, "You're the man. Now follow God." (If you're a husband, you probably know the look I'm talking about. You know how women can be. Then there's that other look they give that says, "I thought I had a man." I don't like that look!)

So I went back to the altar the second time and threw the money down. When I came back to my seat, my wife didn't have anything else to say about an offering. Praise God!

Now for me, at that time and in that situation, to give $200 required a huge amount of trust in God and in my wife. But my wife is not the kind of person to say, "The Lord says this. The Lord says that." In fact, she rarely says that. In twenty years, I haven't heard her say it more than twenty times. So when she speaks, I listen.

Now I had gone to Oklahoma by faith. Everyone told me not to do it. I was twenty-one years old at the time and inexperienced in the area of sowing and reaping. This is what I was expecting to happen: I expected a miracle before the meeting ended. I expected someone to walk up to me, shake my hand, and leave a large sum of money in it! I had heard testimonies of how people acted on the Word of God and — *bam!* — immediately, they got a miracle. Well, we only had $60, and I had to feed my wife and son. I still didn't have a job, and I didn't know when I was going to get one.

Well, the meeting closed. And do you know what happened? Nothing! There was no miracle.

After about a week, the only thing we had left in the house to eat was one TV dinner. Well, since I'm the man, I wasn't going to eat it. I gave it to my wife and son. The next morning I got up to look for a job as usual. I wasn't sitting at home saying, "A job is going to drop into my lap." It doesn't work that way. You have to get out of the house and look. So I was doing all the things I knew to do to find a job.

Now I hadn't eaten the night before, and the gas in my car was almost gone. I mean, I had nothing! We lived in a little mobile home, and our mailbox was out by the road. I had just come home from looking for a job. I pulled up to the mailbox and opened it. There was one letter inside. As I looked at it, I didn't recognize who it was from. Then I remembered the name.

Sometime before we moved to Oklahoma, I had gone to a Kenneth Copeland meeting. I got there very early — long before the doors opened — because I wanted to get a premium seat. I wanted to sit right in front of the man of God. I wanted the anointing to hit me. I was there a couple of hours before the doors opened, but I still didn't get that front row seat. I wound up several rows back sitting next to a businessman.

The businessman said to me, "When you get to Bible school, drop me a line and tell me what the school is like."

So when I got to RHEMA Bible Training Center, I did just that. Then when I saw his letter in the mailbox, I didn't think much about it. I thought he was just writing back.

I went inside our little one-bedroom trailer and opened the letter. Something that looked like a check slid out of the envelope and started falling to the floor, but it never made it! I caught it before it hit the floor, turned it over, and saw that it was a check from this businessman for $600! I started screaming, "Deborah!"

Of course, in that little mobile home, my wife didn't have very far to go. She came around the corner in no time. I showed her the check, and she started screaming. I tell you, I danced all over that mobile home. That $600 was enough money to last us several weeks until I got a job.

That was the first time away from home that I had to stand on the Word of God — that I had to put my trust in God — when my head was saying, "No way!" Now don't get me wrong. There is a time to listen to your head. For example, if you're walking down the middle of the road, and an eighteen-wheeler comes barreling down on you, you'd better listen to your head when it tells your feet to move!

But there's also a time to listen to the Holy Ghost. And as we listened to the Holy Ghost in giving that $200 at RHEMA Day and in the days to come, we saw God supernaturally provide for us while we were students at Bible school. When we graduated, we graduated debt-free. Every bill was paid, and we went into the ministry debt-free.

That was twenty-five years ago, and we have been blessed ever since. But, you see, it started out by putting our trust in God. If you're going to be blessed, you're going to have to put your trust in God. And if this is going to be a year of overflow for you (and that's what we want — overflow blessings), you're going to have to put some overflow trust in God!

Let's look at the *eighth* thing that will cause you to be blessed by God.

Number Eight:
Make a Decision To Live Right

The *eighth* thing you can do to be blessed is *to make a decision to live right*. A person who chooses to live right will be blessed by God.

> **PSALM 106:3**
> 3 **Blessed are they that keep judgment** [or keep the Word of God], **and he that doeth righteousness at all times.**

This verse is talking about the person who makes the decision to live right at all times, in all circumstances. In other words, he lives right and does the right thing whether people are looking or not looking, whether things are going well or badly, whether he understands something or doesn't understand it, or whether he feels like living right or not. He makes the decision, "I'm going to live right, because I'm going to live right!"

Going By Feelings Will Rob You of Blessings

Living right is a decision; it's something you choose to do. Living right is not something you do because you feel like doing it. Feelings come and go. If you were going by feelings, you'd never live right consistently.

Living right is not something you do because all the conditions are favorable for right-living. If that were the case, you'd never live right, because circumstances will always present themselves to you to challenge you. We are to rule and reign over circumstances, not allow them to dictate how we're going to live our lives.

People ask me all the time, "Bishop, will you pray for me that the Lord will make me do right?"

I tell them, "No, I'm not going to pray that. It's unscriptural to pray that. God's not going to make you do right."

Now God will encourage you, but He won't force you to do right. He'll give you the Word to help you do right. He'll make strength and ability available to you. But whether or not you do right is based on a decision that you make. God will not intrude on your decision. You have a right to do whatever you want. God has given you a free will. He has given you the freedom of choice. It's up to you what you decide to do.

Now you can pray for revelation from God, and He will show you the pitfalls that lie ahead of you in life. Jesus said that part of the job of the Holy Ghost is to show you things to come (John 16:13). He will show you what's coming down the road and even show you how to avoid it. But it's up to you to do the avoiding!

Let me give you a couple of illustrations which show that avoiding pitfalls is your responsibility, not God's. If you have had trouble with drinking, then don't go sit in a bar. You should avoid bars. (You should stay out of bars, anyway, but I'm making a particular point here.) If you have trouble with drinking, the last thing you want to do is sit in a bar or run around with people who drink.

I know that sounds obvious, but I've been a pastor too many years to think that people will always do the obvious.

If you have a problem controlling your flesh sexually, why in the world would you go see an X-rated movie? You can't watch a steamy movie of naked people bumping and grinding together without it affecting you. You have to use your brain in some things.

The Holy Ghost will give you a check in your spirit if you're headed some place you're not supposed to be. But He's not going to force you not to go. He will check you, but the responding and the obeying are up to you.

Actually, you know when you're not supposed to be in a particular place or with a particular person. Your flesh may be saying, "Go here. Go there. You're going to get a blessing hanging around that place." But your spirit will be telling you, "No, don't go there," or "Get out of here now!" And you'd better obey your spirit if you want to be blessed by God.

Whenever I counsel with someone who's gotten into trouble, I ask them, "Did something tell you not to do that?"

They usually say, "Yes."

I ask, "Well, why didn't you listen? That wasn't just something talking to you — that was the Holy Ghost!"

Some people can't control their spending. Well, they don't need to be spending all their time at the mall. You know good and well that if you can't control yourself in this area, you need to keep yourself out of department stores! Doing that might help your marriage as well as your wallet!

It's not just some women who have problems with spending too much money. Some men need to watch it too. Keep yourself out of the gun store or the fishing store or wherever you have a problem with spending. Stay out of the store or cut up your credit card!

Your Blessing Includes
Protection for Your Family

God blesses you and your family when you do right and stay undefiled by fleshly excesses.

PROVERBS 20:7
7 **The just man** [the blessed, righteous man] **walketh in his integrity: his children are blessed after him.**

If you want to be blessed by God, never forget who you are as a Christian. You are a son of God, an heir of God, and a joint-heir with Jesus. The Word of God declares that you are the righteousness of God (2 Cor. 5:21). Never forget who you are, and walk in that integrity. Your children's lives depend on it — particularly, if you're a father.

A father is the gateway into everyone else in the family. Satan wants to take out the head first. A father has serious responsibilities. He has to walk in integrity so that his children are not destroyed. A father's seed can be wiped out because of his foolishness.

Now don't misunderstand me. I don't want you to become fearful. There isn't a perfect man or a perfect woman alive. If someone examines you closely, he's going to find a flaw in you. And if you examine someone closely, you're going to find a flaw in him.

Some single people have lists longer than my arm about what they want in a mate! They are believing God for 197 things! It's true; I've seen people's lists. There really should be only five or six things on the list. Yet some women will say, "Well, he has to be six feet, two inches tall with black hair, gray eyes, and has to look like a movie star. And he has to make $200,000 a year." Those women are crazy!

I say to singles, "Why are you asking for all that when you aren't all that?" If a person is asking for "all that," he or she had better be "all that" too! Single women need to look for a man who will be a good protective gateway, someone who will walk in integrity so that their children can be blessed.

Win Your Husband With Your Witness

Now if you're already married and your husband isn't right with God, there's still a way for you and your family to be blessed. Look at First Peter chapter 3.

> **1 PETER 3:1,2**
> **1 Likewise, ye wives, be in subjection to your own husbands; that, if any obey not the word** [talking about those husbands who are not obedient to the Word of God], **THEY ALSO MAY WITHOUT THE WORD BE WON by the conversation** [lifestyle] **of the wives;**
> **2 While they behold your chaste conversation coupled with fear.**

God's Word says that you are supposed to respect your husband even if he's not walking in the Word of God. In fact, these verses in First Peter say that if you will respect him even though he's not walking in the Word and if you will live like a godly woman before him, your life can cause him to turn around and come to the Lord. Your nagging won't do it! Your godly lifestyle and your being a good witness are what will bring your husband in.

Life is full of decisions. You make decisions every day. You can decide to be blessed or you can decide not to be blessed. Remember what Proverbs 20:7 says: "The righteous man walks in his integrity." That's a decision you make. You can decide to follow God, or you can decide not to follow God. You can decide to believe what God said and trust Him, or you can decide not to do that. But the choice is yours. Stop blaming God, saying, "I don't know why God let this happen to me." I do! You got out of the Word. But you can decide to get back in the Word and obey it, and you'll be blessed for your decision.

If you spend enough time with God and His Word, He will always warn you when you need to be warned. As you walk in integrity, He will protect you. Now you can let other things, such as mental reasoning, cause you to make a bad decision at times. But God will always let you know when something is coming down the road that you need to avoid. He's on your side, and He wants to bless you.

Chapter 5
Staying in the Flow Of God's Blessings

I've been talking about eight ways to be blessed by God. Remember that although God has already provided His blessing for us through Christ's death, burial, and resurrection, we must cooperate with God to appropriate and walk in those blessings individually.

What is the *ninth* way in which God can bless us?

Number Nine: Consider the Poor

God is very serious about your helping people who are less fortunate than you. Everyone who is blessed is required by God to reach down and help someone else. The *ninth* thing we can do to be blessed is *to consider the poor.*

Let's read what God has to say about the poor.

PSALM 41:1,2
1 BLESSED is he THAT CONSIDERETH THE POOR: the Lord will deliver him in time of trouble.
2 The Lord will preserve him, and keep him alive: and he shall be BLESSED upon the earth: and

thou wilt not deliver him unto the will of his enemies.

Notice right off the bat, God says that if you consider the poor, He will deliver you in time of trouble (v. 1). Let's read this same passage of Scripture from *The Amplified Bible.*

> **PSALM 41:1,2 (*Amplified*)**
> **1 Blessed (happy, fortunate, to be envied) is he who considers the weak and the poor; the Lord will deliver him in the time of evil and trouble.**
> **2 The Lord will protect him and keep him alive; he shall be called blessed in the land; and You will not deliver him to the will of his enemies.**

Verse 1 in *The Amplified Bible* says, "The Lord will deliver him in the time of evil and trouble." Notice what God promises in verse 2. If you consider the poor, the Lord will protect and preserve you and keep you alive. You shall be blessed on the earth.

So, you see, how you treat the poor has a lot to do with your blessing. If you think only about giving to yourself and you don't ever help others, then when your time of trouble comes, your back won't be covered. You won't be protected.

I'm sure you know of people right now who are in need. Others, you might not be so sure about.

For example, the Lord could be leading you to bless someone, and you're thinking, *He doesn't need money anymore than I do. It would just be 'extra' for him. Well, I could use some 'extra' myself.* But you don't ever know what's going on with someone else. The Lord will lead you to bless certain people, and your head won't necessarily understand.

For instance, the Lord told me one time to give some money to a particular individual, and he looked better than I did. He was wearing alligator shoes, a nice suit, and was driving a late model car! The Lord said to me, "Bless him financially." And I thought, *I don't have that kind of suit or car. That's not God talking; that's the devil talking.*

But it was the Lord talking. It turned out that this man was in serious financial trouble. Now in his case, he was in financial trouble because he had mishandled what he had. He needed instruction on how to handle what he had. (And, eventually, I did teach him.) But first, God wanted me to show love to him and his family.

Sometimes the way in which you get people's attention is to love them. You can say, "I love you" all you want, but when you put some money in their hands, they know you're serious and that there's something different about you.

Your blessing the poor has a lot to do with your being blessed. I don't know anyone who doesn't want to be blessed. I have yet to meet a person who does not want to be blessed. But you must be willing to do what God says you have to do in order to be blessed.

Be a Blessing To *Receive* a Blessing

Let's look again at one of our texts, Proverbs 10:22.

PROVERBS 10:22
22 The blessing of the Lord, it maketh rich, and he addeth no sorrow with it.

The blessing of the Lord makes you rich. It causes you to accumulate. It causes you to prosper. It causes you to be happy. And we know that with His blessing, there will be no sorrow. In other words, God is not schizophrenic! He's not giving you a blessing with one hand and then whacking you with the other!

The will of God is for His children to be blessed. Just as most parents want their children to be blessed, God wants His children to be blessed. And we are the children of God. John 1:12 says, *"But as many as received him, to them gave he power to become the sons of God, even to them that believe on his name."* Now the Greek word for "power" in that verse means *right, privilege, and authority.* God has given us the right, privilege, and authority to become sons of God. And God wants us blessed!

I don't want you to have any doubt about the fact that God wants you blessed. Even if you aren't blessed experientially — even if you're not experiencing the blessings of God right now — it's not because it's not God's will for it to be so in your life. There are things that can inhibit your blessings. Satan will try to stop your blessings. You can also cooperate with the devil, wittingly or unwittingly, and cause your own blessings to be stopped. But you need to know and be convinced of the fact that God wants you blessed.

Number Ten: Be a Giver

Remember we're talking about how to be blessed by God. We mentioned that one way to be blessed by God is to consider the poor. That was number nine. Well, number ten is closely related to number nine. The *tenth* thing we can do to be blessed by God is *to be a giver.*

An individual who is going to be blessed by God must be a giver. Stingy people will not walk in the blessings of God. You have to get rid of that stingy spirit if you want God's blessing on your life. You have to get it out of your house, because stinginess chokes the blessing. On the other hand, liberality releases the blessings of God. Liberality releases happiness and joy.

You know, Jesus said that it is more blessed to give than it is to receive. He said, in effect, "It's more happy for you" (Matt. 10:8; Acts 20:35). Giving releases God's prosperity to you. When you give to others — when you're looking to help someone else other than yourself — you open the door for God to pour out His blessing on you.

Psalm 37:22 says, *"For such as be blessed of him* [the Lord] *shall inherit the earth; and they that be cursed of him shall be cut off."* Now you are either going to be blessed or you're going to be cut off! The individual that is blessed of God inherits the earth. The wicked may have some of the earth in their possession now, but they aren't going to keep it. They're going to be cut off if they don't repent, and the blessed of the Lord are going to inherit the earth.

Get in the 'Giving Flow'!

Some people say, "Well, I don't have anything to give." Wrong! You always have something to give. I can remember when I started out in the things of God, and I didn't have any money. I gave pencils and pens away! Start where you are. I gave shoes away, and I'm not talking about my old beat-up shoes after they became smelly and broken up!

A person who is liberal is someone who stays in the blessing flow. There is a flow of the blessing of God. Proverbs 22:9 says, *"He that hath a bountiful eye shall be blessed; for he giveth of his bread to the poor."* Those who are blessed have a bountiful eye; they are looking for the opportunity to bless others.

You need to ask yourself these questions: Am I a giver? Am I giving? Am I blessing others? Am I setting my sights on others, instead of just on myself? Am I in the giving flow or am I hoarding up?

God told us to bring our tithes, which means a tenth of your increase, into the house of God which is feeding us spiritually. Malachi talks about what will happen if we obey God in this area.

> **MALACHI 3:10**
> 10 Bring ye all the tithes into the storehouse, that there may be meat in mine house, and prove me now herewith, saith the Lord of hosts, if I will not OPEN YOU THE WINDOWS OF HEAVEN, and POUR YOU OUT A BLESSING, that there shall not be room enough to receive it.

God said that He would pour you out a blessing, and you wouldn't even have enough room to receive it. But you have to be a giver. That's God's system. God is not asking you to do something that He doesn't do or hasn't done Himself. John 3:16 says, "For God so loved the world that He gave His Son." God gave His Son to us. And He expects us to give our lives to Him — and that means everything about our lives, not just bits and pieces of it here and there.

People who aren't givers — people who are stingy about their money, their time, their talents, their service to God, and so forth — are people who won't stay blessed. You have to be a giver to be a receiver. And don't worry about someone else who's getting blessed because of his giving. God has plenty of blessings to go around. His blessings are like a river. They flow from one place to another and bless that place. Then they flow to the next place and bless that place too. So you know that when you see So-and-so getting blessed, you can praise God because you know the flow is heading your way!

Sometimes people become a dam, so to speak. They stop the flow of the blessings of God. They build walls so that the blessings can't go anywhere else. They try to hold them just for themselves. But it doesn't work that way. You can be a dam for a while, but that water is going to find a way around you. You have to be a giver if you want to be blessed by God. You have to stay in the giving flow.

There are sacrifices involved in giving to others. For example, you might have to give up some of your prayer time for your family and pray for others. Don't be like the man who said, "Lord, my name is Jimmy. I'll take all you'll 'gimme.' Bless me, my wife, my two kids — us four and no more"! You can't be that way and stay in the flow of giving and receiving. You have to be an individual who will give of yourself, your time, your prayers, and your money.

Keep the blessings flowing to yourself. God said, "I'll open you the windows of Heaven and pour you out a blessing" (Mal. 3:10). When you bless others, blessings come your way. That's God's way.

God Said, 'Prove Me'

God said in Malachi 3:10 to prove Him, to put Him the test. Other areas in the Word of God say, "Don't try God." But when it comes to giving, God said, "Prove Me, or test Me, and see if I will not open the windows of Heaven for you."

Now the Hebrew word for "windows" is the same word used during the time of Noah and the flood. When it rained, the Bible says, "The windows of Heaven opened" (Gen. 7:11). And of course, it rained so much that it washed out the whole earth except for Noah's family and those who were in the ark. Now that was a serious rain — forty days and forty nights of the biggest thunderstorm you could ever imagine! The windows of Heaven opened. This is the same Hebrew word that's used in Malachi.

In other words, God is saying, "I will open unto you the windows [the floodgates] of Heaven" (Mal. 3:10). Now that's a mighty big window! That's a window big enough to wash away all of your poverty! That's a window big enough to wash away all of your fears! It's big enough to wash away all of your bills! It's big enough to wash away all that's binding you!

Debt Is Bondage

There is a reason why the Bible says that the borrower is servant to the lender (Prov. 22:7). You see, lenders will try to do whatever they want. They'll try to put all kinds of conditions on you when you borrow from them. They'll try to control your life, and they feel they have a right to do it, because you're using their money.

Do you want to get out of debt as soon as possible? There are a number of ways to do it. One way is to stop all your excess spending. I am referring to all the spending that the Holy Ghost isn't leading you to do.

Another way is to sow — in tithes and offerings. God says concerning the tithe, "Put Me to the test; prove Me now. See if I will not open the windows of Heaven and pour you out a blessing that there shall not be enough room to hold it." When you don't have room enough to hold the blessing, then it will flow out of that room. That's overflow! God will keep pouring out on you until you don't have any more room.

There's Financial Freedom
In the Overflow!

When you don't have any more room, you have to get "bigger." If there's not enough room in your barn, then you have to get a bigger barn. If there's not enough room in your house, you have to get a bigger house. If the trunk in your car is not big enough, you have to get a bigger car! And regardless of how big you get, God still says the same thing: "Whatever size it is, I will pour you out a blessing that there is not room enough to receive it." That means it just keeps on going. It's continual overflow!

Let's look in First Kings to see how we can get in the overflow.

> **1 KINGS 17:8-12**
> **8 And the word of the Lord came unto him, saying,**
> **9 Arise, get thee to Zarephath, which belongeth to Zidon, and dwell there: behold, I have commanded a widow woman there to sustain thee.**
> **10 So he arose and went to Zarephath. And when he came to the gate of the city, behold, the widow woman was there gathering of sticks: and he called to her, and said, Fetch me, I pray thee, a little water in a vessel, that I may drink.**
> **11 And as she was going to fetch it, he called to her, and said, Bring me, I pray thee, a morsel of bread in thine hand.**
> **12 And she said, As the Lord thy God liveth, I have not a cake** [There are a lot of people in this "have not" category], **but an handful of meal in a barrel, and a little oil in a cruse: and, behold, I am gathering two sticks, that I may go in and dress it for me and my son, that we may eat it, and die.**

Well, the condition of this widow woman in Zarephath sure wasn't overflow. It sure wasn't abundance. In fact, it was poverty, and poverty is not a blessing from God.

When I was growing up in the church, it seemed that preachers taught that the poorer you were, the holier you were. But I noticed that being poor didn't necessarily make you holy. Now it may have produced something "holey" — such as holes in the bottom of your shoes! But being poor isn't what makes you holy.

Notice what the prophet Elijah said to this woman. She had just told him that she and her son didn't have enough to share. In fact, they only had enough for one last meal. They were going to eat it and die. You would think the prophet, after he heard that, would have backed off and said, "Oh, I'm sorry. I must have missed God. He told me you were supposed to sustain me. I must have heard wrong, or I've got the wrong woman." Instead, what did the prophet Elijah say to her? He said, "Fear not" (1 Kings 17:13). He wasn't moved by her lack.

Don't Let Pressure
Get You Out of the Flow

When you are in a position of "have not," the first thing you have to do is decide not to give in to the pressure or the fear of being wiped out financially. You have to control your fear, so you can get back over into the flow and do what God wants you to do.

Some people shake like a leaf because of bad news, because of the "have-not" reports that are hitting them right and left. You may have some "have nots" on your desk right now. You may have received some "have-not" phone calls. Your spouse may be talking to you about the "have nots," and it's producing pressure on you — pressure on your body, your psyche, and your spirit.

Then fear comes along and says, "What are you going to do?" Well, I'll tell you what you're going to do. You are going to fear not! Fear is just the opposite of faith. Fear is what activates Satan. Faith is what activates God!

Elijah said to the widow woman, "Fear not. Go and make me a little cake first" (1 Kings 17:13). Many people would say, "Oh, that greedy preacher. The woman just told him that's all she had, and he wants to take it from her."

Then Elijah said to her, "I know this is all you've got, but give me what you have." That sounds bad. The media would be jumping all over a preacher who did that today. That's because they have no understanding of how God operates.

Let's read what the Lord then said to this woman.

1 KINGS 17:14
14 For thus saith the Lord God of Israel, The barrel of meal shall not waste, neither shall the cruse of oil fail, until the day that the Lord sendeth rain upon the earth.

What was God saying? He was saying that every time she reached into the barrel — the same barrel that was empty previously — and took the meal out, the hole she made was going to "fill up" again. Every time she poured out oil from the cruse — the same one that was empty before she obeyed God — the cruse would fill up and be full when she set it down again.

How does this relate to us today? God isn't saying that He is going to give you twenty-five barrels of meal. He isn't saying that He is going to give you an eighteen-wheeler truck full of oil that should last you for the next three years or so. But He is saying that the flow of His blessing won't stop as long as you are obeying Him and staying in the giving flow.

Never Stop Sowing —
In the Good Times or the Bad

Overflow can come in many different ways. When I was a Bible student some twenty years ago, God kept having me sow my little bit of meal that I had. I didn't have much. In fact, most of the time, I almost had nothing! But the entire time I was at Bible school, I was sowing.

As I mentioned previously, when I arrived at Bible school, I was already in debt because of some circumstances that happened years before. When my wife and I first got married, I changed jobs. And there was a six-day period during which we were uninsured. And, coincidentally, my wife got ill and wound up in the hospital during those six days. If it had been before or after that six-day period, we would have been covered by medical insurance. But it happened right in the window of the six days.

The devil knows exactly what he's doing when he brings pressure. I'm sure you know how fast medical bills can accumulate. Just one day in the hospital could cost you thousands of dollars, depending on what procedures you undergo. So the debt we had was a result of those medical bills.

But the entire time I'm in Bible school, God was having me sow seed into the prophet of God, Rev. Kenneth E. Hagin. What I sowed really wasn't very much, but every thirty or forty days, we experienced a financial miracle. I never seemed to have money in my pocket, yet when I went into my pocket, I had the money I needed.

When I graduated from Bible school, all of my bills were paid! They were paid supernaturally. Then God sent me into the ministry full time with all my debt wiped out. I still don't know exactly how they all got cancelled out, and I don't care! But I do know this one thing: God opened up a window of Heaven and blessed me.

So Elijah told this woman that her barrel of meal and cruse of oil would not fail until the day the Lord sent the rain upon the earth. So what did she do? She acted; she obeyed the word of the Lord through the prophet Elijah. She went and made that cake and brought it into the man of God first. And then she made a cake for her and her son.

But instead of dying, every time this woman made another cake, there was more left for even more cakes. Her supply just kept going and going and going until the famine ended and she no longer needed that kind of a miracle.

How long will your miracle last? As long as you need it. God will stretch it out as long as necessary. Now I don't need that kind of a miracle right now. I'm not a poor man; I'm a blessed man. But as I continue to be liberal and bless other people, God is still opening windows and pouring out blessings.

And I have to give blessings away because I have so much and because I want to stay in God's giving flow.

God Will Protect and Defend Your Harvest

You can be blessed by God by being an individual who gives. God said, "I will open the windows of Heaven and pour you out a blessing that there shall not be room enough to receive it, and I will rebuke the devourer for your sake" (Mal. 3:10,11). When God said that He would rebuke the devourer, He meant that your harvest would not be destroyed. Let's read verses 11 and 12.

> MALACHI 3:11,12
> 11 And I will rebuke the devourer for your sakes, and he shall not destroy the fruits of your ground; neither shall your vine cast her fruit before the time in the field, saith the Lord of hosts.
> 12 And all nations shall call you blessed: for ye shall be a delightsome land, saith the Lord of hosts.

What does God mean when he says, "Neither shall your vine cast her fruit before the time"? He means you won't get out of sequence. You won't get out of time. In other words, when it's time for you to harvest, you're going to harvest. When your crop gets ripe for picking, you're going to be able to pick it and fill up your basket.

Then He said, "All nations shall call you blessed." Your family members will call you blessed. Your enemy will call you blessed. Your co-workers will call you blessed.

Other people will call you blessed because they will see something happening to you, and they will know that it can't be you that's doing it. They will see that it has to be a "higher power," as the world likes to call it. But they are right! There is a higher Power who is higher than your debt, your fear, or your discouragement! This Power is more powerful than the devil, who has tried to hold you down. This Power is God Almighty! And He will pour you out a blessing that overflows in your life until you don't have enough room to hold it all. You'll have to build a second barn! Then you'll have to build a third barn and a fourth and so on. You'll have to build a bigger church or ministry.

That's the God I know! If we live right — if we are holy before God and do what He tells us to do when we're supposed to do it — we can count on God to do what He said He would do! He's not a man that He should lie (Num. 23:19). He's not lying to you! He said that it is your time! It is your season! It is His will for you to be blessed coming in, blessed going out, blessed in the city, and blessed in the field (Deut. 28:1-8).

The day I walked on the property which our church now owns, the head officer over the property said to me, "You're Keith Butler." The Holy Ghost had sent me to go see him, and when I walked into the room, that's what he said.

I said, "Yes, sir."

He said, "You're the man I'm supposed to sell this property to."

I said, "I'm the man."

That was God's blessings. And in your own life, people will say to you, "I don't know why, but this belongs to you! This job belongs to you! This opportunity belongs to you!"

You will say, "I'm the one! I'm the blessed of the Lord!"

God will get involved in your affairs. He'll get involved in your business. He'll get involved in your marriage. He'll bring healing to your body. He'll get into every area of your life. And when God gets in, who's going to elbow Him out?

That's the blessing of the Lord. So don't ever stop sowing. Stay in the giving flow. Look for someone to give something to every day. It doesn't matter if it's just ten cents. Bless someone with something every day. Constantly sow, and constantly receive. Ecclesiastes 11:1 says, "Cast your bread out on the water, and it will come back on every wave."

God Has Wave After Wave Of Blessing for You!

When you first start doing this, it comes back on every wave, but it comes back in a small portion. But when you consistently do this for a long time, you come to the place where it's not just morsels on the waves. No, your blessings are coming back to you in battleships. They're coming back on tanker boats. And behind that wave is another tanker! The blessings just keep coming!

I have had ministers (particularly those who knew me twenty-five years ago) say to me, "How did you get to where you are today? How did you get from nobody with nothing to being so blessed by God?"

I say, "I'm blessed by God because I fear the Lord. I delight greatly in His commandments. And His commandments say I'm blessed. I'm prosperous. I'm happy."

Well, there are a number of things that have caused me to be blessed, but one of them is giving. Our ministry is a sowing ministry. And when I go to another ministry to speak, I don't go to collect an offering; I go to *give* an offering. I don't go empty-handed. I go with a big check! I want to be a blessing, and I want to get in and *stay* in the flow of God's blessings!

Chapter 6
Be Devoted to God
And Abound in His Blessings!

As Christians, we know or should know that God has blessed us in Christ. For example, Ephesians 1:3 says, *"Blessed be the God and Father of our Lord Jesus Christ, who HATH BLESSED us with all spiritual blessings in heavenly places in Christ."* It's one thing to know God has blessed us, but it's another thing entirely to tap in to those blessings and make them ours experientially. Thank God, we can learn how to cooperate with God and enjoy the fullness of His blessings in this life.

I've already covered ten things we can do to be blessed by God. Let's look at the *eleventh* thing we can do.

Number Eleven:
Be a Person of Faithfulness

The *eleventh* thing you can do to be blessed is *to be a person of faithfulness.* Who is a faithful man or woman? The word "faithfulness" means *firmness, security, fidelity, and truth.* A faithful man is one

who will tell the truth regardless of the conse-
quences. A faithful man is someone you can count
on. He will stand firm and secure on his convictions. He will live the truth.

Proverbs 28:20 says, *"A faithful man shall*
abound with blessings: but he that maketh haste to
be rich shall not be innocent." A person who
"maketh haste to be rich" is willing to do anything
to anyone in order to get ahead. He is not faithful.
He is not living the truth. And he will not be
blessed by God.

A faithful man will stick with his wife. And a
faithful woman will stick with her husband. And if
a woman doesn't have a husband, she won't mess
with anyone else's husband if she's faithful.

Some women are not faithful to God or man.
They don't fear God, and they don't live by the
truth. For example, you may never see a particular
woman dress up, but then one day she's dressed up
nicely. Every hair is in place. She has on expensive
clothing, and it's form-fitting, because she's been
working out. Sometimes that means that woman
has her eye on a man somewhere. (You know, some
women can be walking around in curlers, but when
they see a man they want, they'll get to the beauty
shop every day until they get him. Then the curlers

come back again!) That man she has her eye on should be single, but that's not always the case.

This can happen even in church. You might always see the same sister positioned in the same place, dressed sharp and waiting for the pastor as he walks by. She says, "Hi, Pastor" in a seductive way. Then she says, "Will you pray for me today?"

I've actually had that happen to me. I say, "No, I'm not going to pray for you. I'm going to have one of my lady ministers pray for you."

A seductive, unfaithful woman might say, "Oh, pastor, I just love your preaching. Do you make visitations yourself? I don't want one of the other pastors to come to my house. I just know you have a word for me."

I don't counsel women anymore, but I remember one time I was counseling a sister, and as I was looking down, turning the pages in the Bible to find what God had to say about her situation, she was undressing! I said, "Turn in your Bible to...," and when I looked up, she was naked from the waist up!

Of course, I threw her out of my office. You know, the devil is crazy! But, usually, when he sends someone your way to try to trip you up, he or she will be well-endowed, as this woman was. Your flesh might say, "Whoa!" But your spirit will say, "Uh-oh." And you're going to have to make a decision right then as to whether or not you'll be faithful. A faithful man will be blessed. A faithful man abounds with blessings. That means that blessings will come to him from everywhere. And a faithful man is secure and firm in his convictions. He knows how to say, "No!"

Let's look at the *twelfth* way to be blessed by God.

Number Twelve: Seek God First

Matthew 6:33 says, *"But SEEK YE FIRST the kingdom of God, and his righteousness; and all these things shall be added unto you."* The *twelfth* thing we can do to be blessed is to *seek God first.*

A blessed man seeks God first before he does anything else. Psalm 37:23 says, *"The steps of a good man are ordered by the Lord: and he delighteth in his way."* A blessed man allows his steps to be ordered by God.

You need to seek the face of God first before you make certain moves and changes in your life. For example, you may be offered the promotion of a lifetime, but you need to seek God before you just automatically take it. Pray and ask God if you should take the promotion. He may want you to wait for something else. Allow Him to order your steps. If your steps are ordered by God, you can't go wrong. You will be blessed.

Number Thirteen: Give God Your All

The thirteenth thing you need to do to be blessed by God is to give God your all. You really can't take this step until you've taken step number twelve, because in order to give God everything, you have to seek Him with your whole heart. Psalm 119 says, *"Blessed are the undefiled in the way, who walk in the law of the Lord. Blessed are they that keep his testimonies, and that seek him with the whole heart"* (vv. 1,2). You'll be blessed if you give God everything — if you give Him your all.

Run after God. Run after His Word. Seek Him and hunger for Him daily. The Bible says, *"BLESSED are they which do hunger and thirst after righteousness: for they shall be filled"* (Matt. 5:6). Seek the Lord with your whole heart — with everything that's in you — and you'll be blessed!

In review, numbers eleven through thirteen show us three things we can do to be blessed by God: 1) *Be a person of faithfulness*; 2) *seek God first*; and 3) *give God your all*. What is the *fourteenth* thing we can do to be blessed by God?

Number Fourteen:
Give Your Life to Him

The *fourteenth* thing we can do to be blessed is closely connected with the last three steps, and it is *to give your life to God*. If you want to live in the blessings of God, say to Him, "Lord, everything about me — everything I have, all my desires and ambitions, and all my will — I submit to You, because I'm Yours. I give You my whole life. Send me where You want to send me. Do with me what You will."

Now a person who will sincerely put himself in a position like this before God cannot help but be blessed! You may say to the Lord, "Lord, now You know my character. You know my flaws and my weaknesses. But I give my life to You. I'll go where You say go and do what You say do." But He will give you the chance to show Him you mean it.

Many have accepted Jesus Christ as Savior, and they might even call Him their Lord and Savior. But not nearly as many have really accepted Him as Lord and have really given their whole life to Him. They are forfeiting many of the blessings of

God, but the person who gives his life to God is the person who'll be blessed!

Finally, let's look at the *fifteenth* thing we can do to be blessed by God.

Number Fifteen: Walk in Love

The *fifteenth* thing we need to do to be blessed by God is to *walk in love*. The Word of God has much to say on this subject, and entire books have been written about it.

What does in mean to walk in love? Well, practically speaking, instead of getting into a tit-for-tat fight or argument with someone, just walk in love! Don't argue and fight with people. Don't get over into strife. Strife will hinder the blessings of God in your life, but love never fails (1 Cor. 13:8).

The following is just one scripture that illustrates that we need to walk in love to be blessed.

> **1 PETER 3:9**
> 9 Not rendering evil for evil, or railing for railing: but contrariwise blessing; knowing that ye are thereunto called, THAT YE SHOULD INHERIT A BLESSING.

If God said to walk in love — and He has said it over and over again in His Word — then you *can* walk in love! And if you will do it, you will inherit His blessing!

Let's review all fifteen things we can do to be blessed by God.

1. Learn how to endure temptation.

2. Begin with the Word of God.

3. Act on the Word of God.

4. Listen to God.

5. Walk in the fear of God.

6. Don't walk in the counsel of the ungodly.

7. Put your complete confidence in God.

8. Make a decision to live right.

9. Consider the poor.

10. Be a giver.

11. Be a person of faithfulness.

12. Seek God first.

13. Give God your all.

14. Give your life to God.

15. Walk in love.

In this chapter, I've covered aspects of being devoted to God as an avenue to being blessed by Him. But, really, all fifteen ways to be blessed illustrate characteristics of being consecrated, dedicated, and sold out to God.

For example, you won't endure temptation, tests, and trials — the trying of your faith — if you're not sold out to God's Word, knowing that God is faithful who promised and that what He promised, He is able also to perform. And you won't begin with the Word of God if you're not convinced that God and His Word are One and that His Word is the beginning and ending of your blessing — your source of faith and the power with which God brings His blessings to pass.

The blessings of God are for anyone who will obey God and His Word and follow Him wholeheartedly — for anyone who is willing to pay that price. There is a price to pay. Yes, God made His blessings available to us in His plan of redemption which was consummated by the Lord Jesus Christ. But as my spiritual father says, those blessings aren't going to just fall on you like ripe cherries off a tree. There's something you're going to have to do. The question is, are you willing to pay the price?

There is a way to be blessed by God beyond your highest dreams, goals, desires, and imagination. And God has not hidden the way from you. He wants you to be blessed more than you want to be blessed! The key lies in your devotion to Him and His Word.

Other Titles By Keith A. Butler Sr.
And Word of Faith Publishing

Bishop Keith A. Butler

A Seed Will Meet Any Need	BK003
Hell: You Don't Want To Go There	BK005
Making Room for Yourself	BK007
Angels — God's Servants for You	BK010
The Last Week of Jesus	BK020
Success Strategies From Heaven	BK001 (Harrison House, Inc.)
What On Earth Are We Here For?	BK002 (Harrison House, Inc.)

Min. Deborah L. Butler

Establishing Godly Relationships Through Marriage and Family	BK012

Rev. Keith A. Butler II

God's Plan for the Single Saint	BK006